billy. La la la

la la la la la

oo. La la la la

la la la la la

a doo. La la

om. La la la

la la la la

a collection of
CONCRETE poems

selected by PAUL B. JANECZKO

illustrated by CHRIS RASCHKA

A POKE IN THE I

```
P A U L J A N E C Z K O
P A U L J A N E C H H K O O
P A U L J A A E C H H K O O
P A U I J A A E C H H K O
P A U I J A A E C H H K A
P H U I J A A E C H H K A A
P H U I J R A E C H H K A A
C H U I J R A E C H K A A
C H U I J R A S C H H K A A
C H U I J R A S C H H K A
C H R I J R A S C H K A A
C H R I J R A S C H K A A
C H R I S R A S C H K A
```

CANDLEWICK PRESS
CAMBRIDGE, MASSACHUSETTS

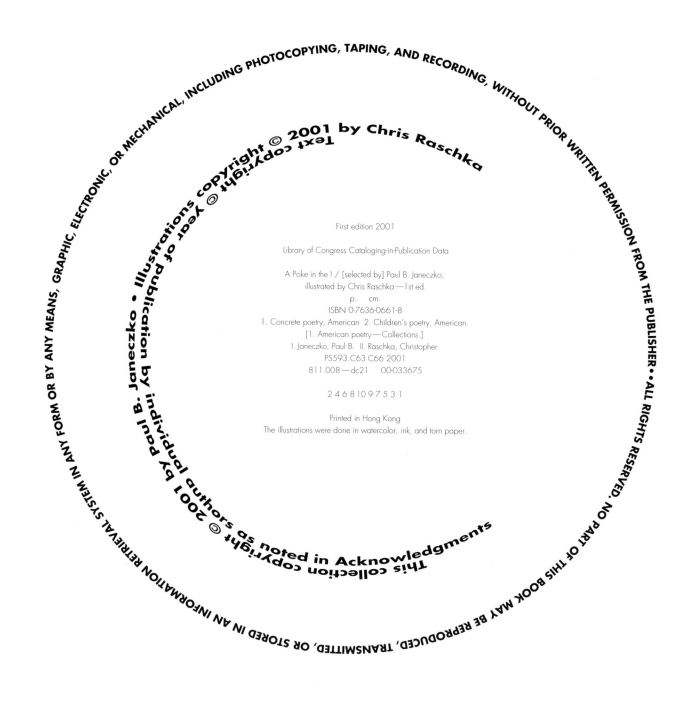

First edition 2001

Library of Congress Cataloging-in-Publication Data

A Poke in the I / [selected by] Paul B. Janeczko;
illustrated by Chris Raschka—1st ed.
p.   cm.
ISBN 0-7636-0661-8
1. Concrete poetry, American 2. Children's poetry, American.
[1. American poetry—Collections.]
I. Janeczko, Paul B. II. Raschka, Christopher.
PS593.C63 C66 2001
811.008—dc21   00-033675

2 4 6 8 10 9 7 5 3 1

Printed in Hong Kong
The illustrations were done in watercolor, ink, and torn paper.

Candlewick Press · 2067 Massachusetts Avenue · Cambridge, Massachusetts 02140

To the memory of my father,
Frank Janeczko (1914–2000)
This one's for you, Pop.
Thanks for everything.
P. B. J.

To Richard Foster
C. R.

TABLE
OF
CONTENTS

Notes from the Editor

Concrete poems are different from regular poems; in fact, they're a lot more playful, as you might guess from the title of this book. What are they, you ask? Well, a concrete poem can be as simple as a single word, like STOWAWAY from Robert Carola. That word becomes a poem because of the unusual way the type is placed on the page. A concrete poem can also be a selection of words arranged into a particular shape, like "Eskimo Pie" by John Hollander. The arrangement of letters or words on the page, the typefaces chosen, and the way space is used, add meaning to the poem beyond that contained in the actual words. Look at Robert Froman's "Easy Diver," for example, where the poem *is* the pigeon.

Concrete poems are often hard to read aloud (try "Crickets" from Aram Saroyan), although sometimes they are irresistible, like Helen Chasin's fourteen-line "Joy Sonnet in a Random Universe" — sh-boom, sh-boom!

Finally, these visually arresting poems are accompanied by Chris Raschka's stunning illustrations, which have a poetry all their own. So, turn the page for a dazzling, bewitching tour of thirty concrete poems from some of the world's finest visual poets and prepare for A Poke in the I.

A SEEING POEM

Robert Froman

A SEEING POEM HAPPENS WHEN WORDS TAKE A SHAPE THAT HELPS THEM TO TURN ON A LIGHT IN SOMEONE'S MIND

2

go

ng!

A WEAK POEM

(To be read lying down)

Roger McGough

Oh dear, this poem is very weak

It can hardly stand up straight

Which comes from eating junk food

And going to bed too late.

4

a poem moves down a page

faster than a novel

CAT CHAIR

Chris Raschka

cat

Pigeon on the roof.

Dives.

Go-

ing

fa-

st.

G O I N G   T O

HIT HARD!

Opens   wings.

Softly,   gently,

down.

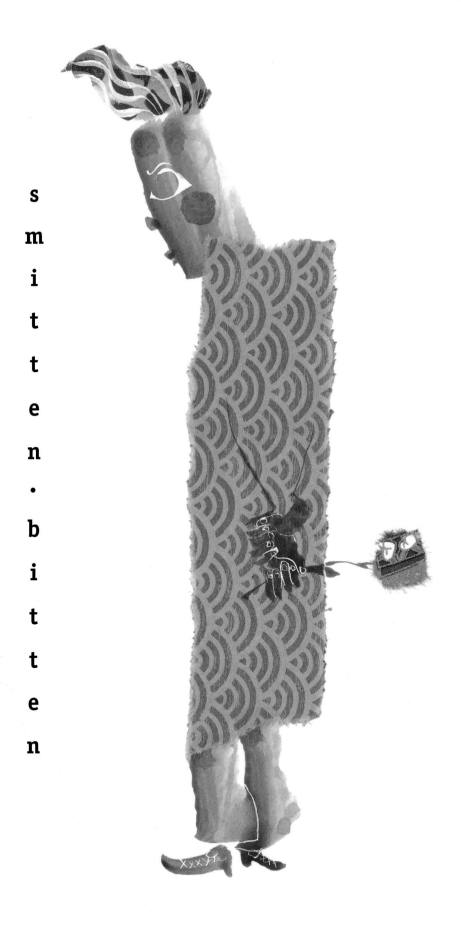

smitten.bitten

STOWAWAY

Robert Carola

eyeleveleye

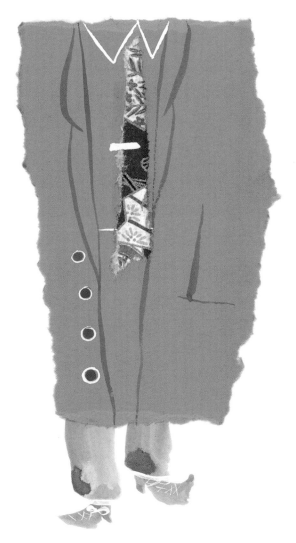

Ronald Johnson

I
NEED
CONTACT

L E N S E S

like I need a poke in the eye

John Hegley

SKIPPING ROPE SPELL

John Agard

Turn rope turn, Don't trip my feet, Turn rope turn, For my skipping feet.

Turn rope turn, Turn in the air, Turn on the ground, Turn round and round,

12

Turn rope turn, Turn to the north, Turn to the south, But please rope, please, Don't make me out.

One for your high, One for your low, Turn rope turn, Not too fast, Not too slow.

13

QUEUE
Sylvia Cassedy

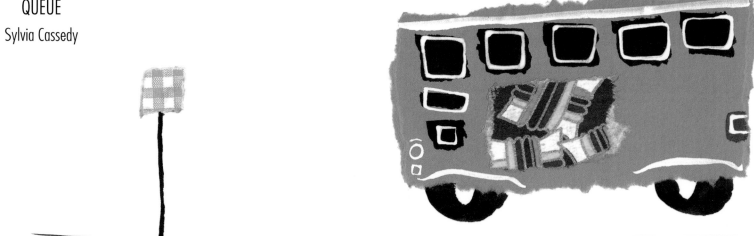

The
life
of
this
queue
depends
only
on
you.
One
step
out
of
line
    and
    it
    all
    breaks
    in
    two.

M
E
R
G
A F
T R
IFNIGC

Allen Jones

ESKIMO PIE

John Hollander

I shall
never pretend
to have forgotten
such loves as those
that turned the dying
brightness at an end of
a childs afternoon into
preludes To an evening of
lamplight To a night dark
with blanketing To mornings
of more and more There deep
in the old ruralities of play
the frosted block with papery
whisps still stuck to it kissed
me burningly as it arose out of
dry icy stillnesses And there now
again I taste first its hard then
its soft Now I am into the creamy
treasure which to have tasted is to
have begun to lose to the heat of a
famished sun But O if I break faith
with you poor dreadful popsicle may
my mouth forget warm rains a tongue
must Pauillac cool skin all tastes
I see
sweet
drops
slide
along
a hot
stick
It is
a sad
sorry
taste
which
never
comes
to an
end

POPSICLE

Joan Bransfield Graham

Popsicle
Popsicle
tickle
tongue fun
licksicle
sticksicle
please
don't run
dripsicle
slipsicle
melt, melt
tricky
stopsicle
plopsicle
hand all
sticky

17

NO PRETENDING

Robert Froman

DANDELION, NO
BRIGHT DANDELION

You

are

not

for

any-

thing,

You

just

are.

she loves me

she loves me not

she loves

she loves me

she

she loves

she

SKY DAY DREAM

Robert Froman

WITH THEM

COULD FLY OFF

I WISHED THAT I

INTO THE SKY

FLY OFF

SOME CROWS

ONCE I SAW

CRICKETS

Aram Saroyan

```
crickets
crickess
cricksss
cricssss
crisssss
crsssss
csssssss
ssssssss
ssssssts
sssskets
sssckets
ssickets
srickets
crickets
```

21

THE SALMON
Douglas Florian

Could do with legs!
Just think what we
Our pearly eggs.
Upstream we spawn
We somersault!
We vault!
We jump!
Our leaps astound!
We bound!
We spring!

22

You'll see a saw

Upon my jaw,

But I can't cut

A two-by-four,

Or build a bed,

Or frame a door.

My splendid saw's

For goring fishes—

I eat them raw

And don't do dishes.

SWAN AND SHADOW

John Hollander

```
                    Dusk
                 Above the
            water hang the
                    loud
                    flies
                 Here
                 O so
                 gray
                 then
                 What        A  pale signal will appear
                 When        Soon before its shadow fades
                 Where        Here in this pool of opened eye
                 In us      No Upon us As at  the very edges
               of  where we take shape in the dark air
                 this object  bares its  image awakening
                    ripples of recognition that will
                    brush darkness up into light
  even after this bird this hour both drift by atop the perfect sad instant now
                    already passing out of sight
                    toward yet-untroubled reflection
                 this image bears its object darkening
                 into memorial shades Scattered bits of
                 light        No of water Or something across
                 water          Breaking up No Being regathered
                 soon           Yet by then a swan will have
                    gone                Yes out of mind into what
                    vast
                    pale
                    hush
                    of a
                    place
                    past
            sudden dark as
                 if a swan
                    sang
```

24

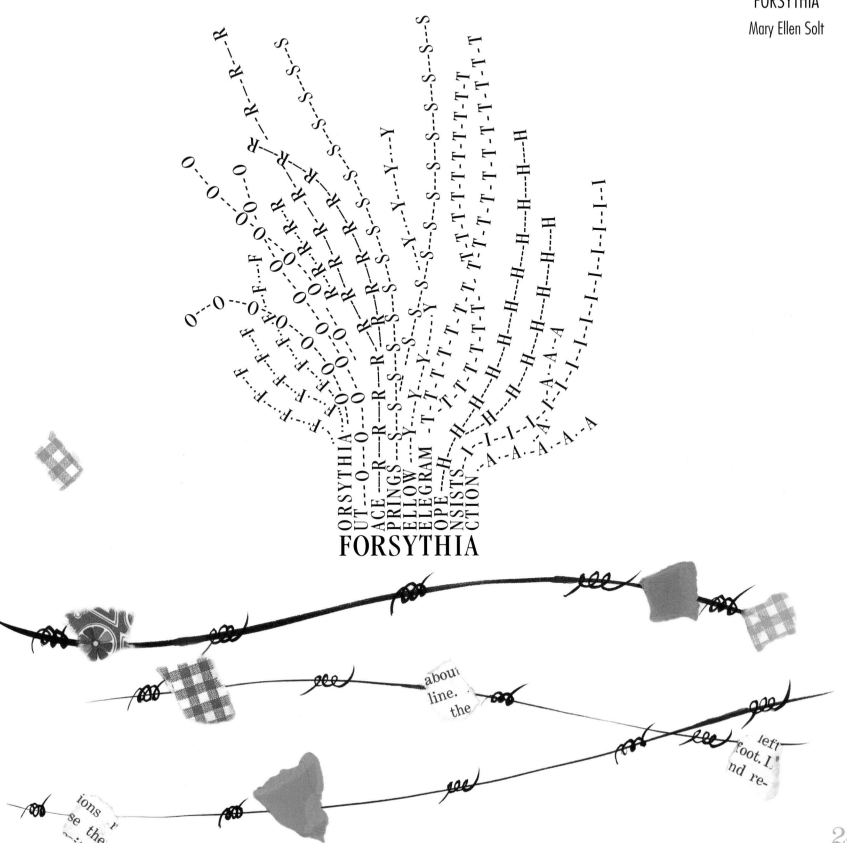

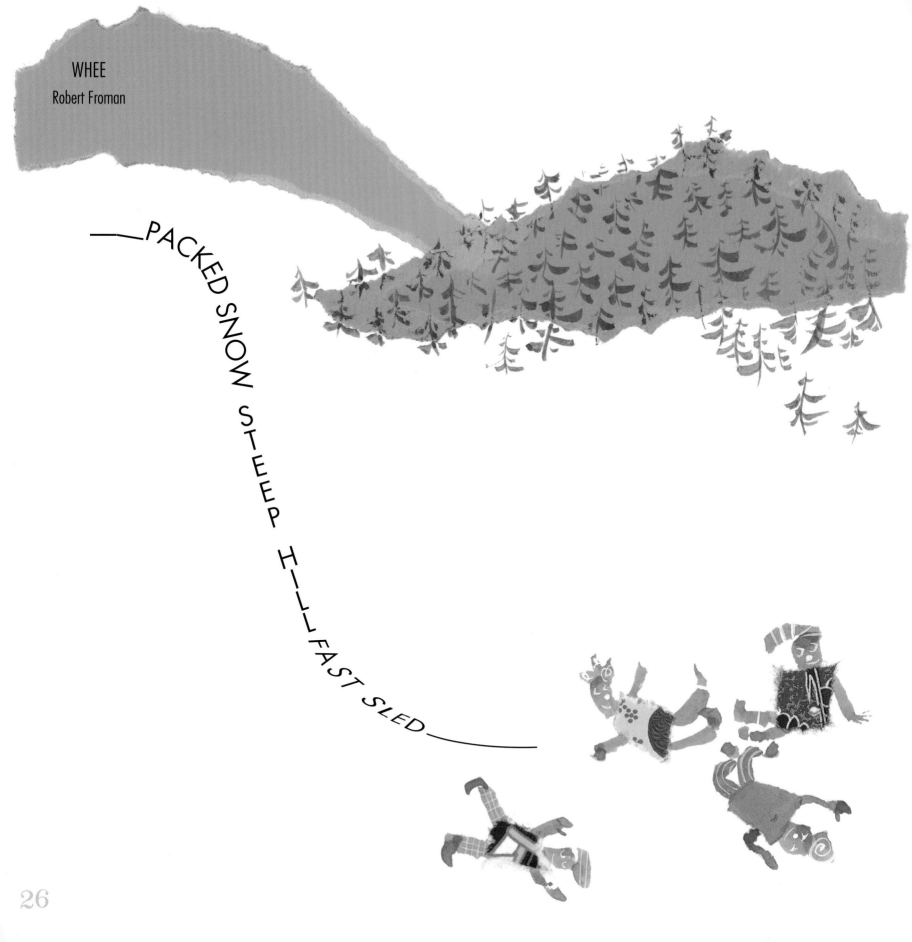

WHEE
Robert Froman

PACKED SNOW STEEP HILL FAST SLED

26

as
big as
ball as round
as sun . . . I tug
and pull you when
you run and when
wind blows I
say polite
ly
H
O
L
D
M
E
T
I
G
H
T
L
Y

BALLOON
Colleen Thibaudeau

GIRAFFE

Maureen W. Armour

A
GIRAFFE
I
S
S
O
T
A
L
L
A
N
D
HIS HEAD IS SO
FAR ABOVE HIS LEGS
HE PROBABLY CAN'T SEE

HIS ADORABLE   TOES OR ANYTHING   ELSE BELOW HIS   KNEES AND ELBOWS

28

a   a   a   a   a

c   c   c   c

r   r   r   r   r

o   o   o   o

b   b   b   b   b

a   a   a   a

t   t   t   t   t

s   s   s   s

t   t   t   t   t

a   a   a   a

b   b   b   b   b

o   o   o   o

r   r   r   r   r

c   c   c   c

a   a   a   a   a

Ian Hamilton Finlay

29

Tennis

game I

for hours

neck won't

is a

could watch

but my

let me

31

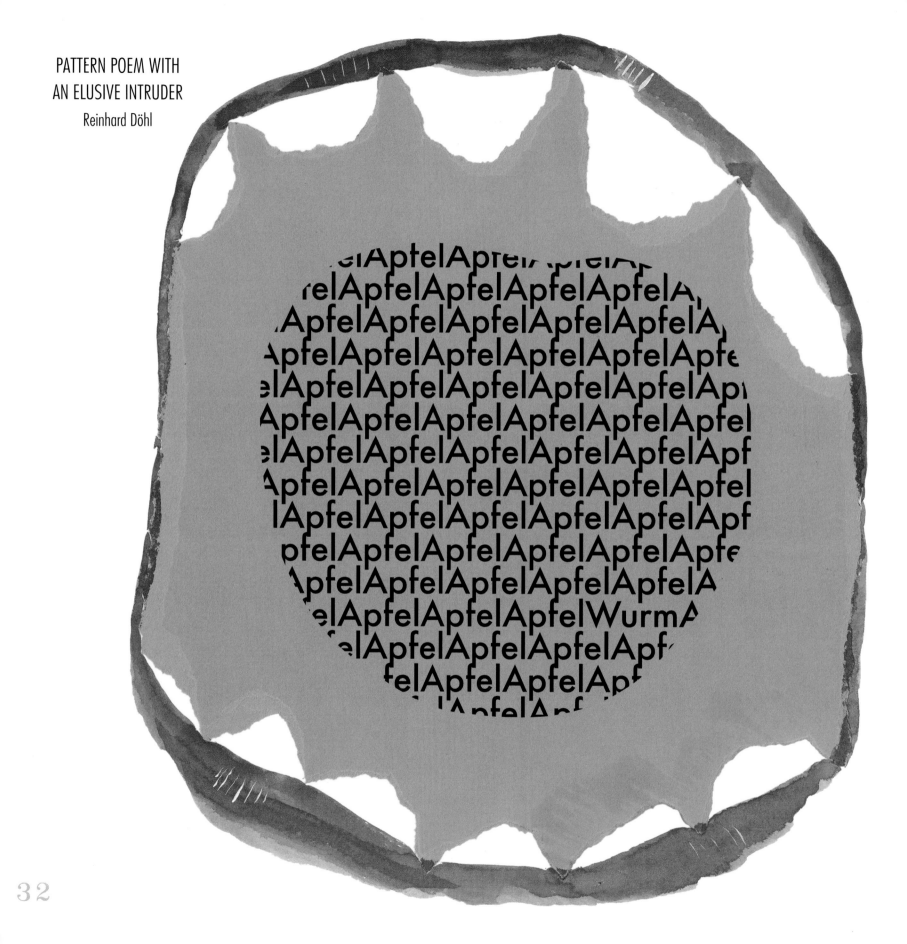

PATTERN POEM WITH
AN ELUSIVE INTRUDER
Reinhard Döhl

32

Sometimes I'm happy: la la la la la la la
la la la la la la la la la la la la la la la la
la la la la. Tum tum ti tum. La la la la la la
la la la la la la la la la la la la la la la la.
Hey nonny nonny. La la la la la la la la la
la la la la la la la la la la la. Vo do di o do.
Poo poo pi doo. La la la la la la la la la la
la la la la la la la la la la la la la la la la
la la. Whack a doo. La la la la la la la. Sh-
boom, sh-boom. La la la la la la la la la
la la la la la la la la la la la la la la la la
la la. Dum di dum. La la la la la la la la
la la la la la la la la la. Tra la la. Tra la la
la la la la la la la la la la. Yeah yeah yeah.

ACKNOWLEDGMENTS

"A Seeing Poem" by Robert Froman, from *Seeing Things* by Robert Froman, published by Thomas Y. Crowell, 1974. Copyright © 1974 by Robert Froman. Reprinted by permission of Katherine Froman.

"Visual Soundpoem" by Edwin Morgan, from *Collected Poems* by Edwin Morgan, published by Carcanet Press Limited, Manchester, England, 1996. Copyright © 1971 by Carcanet Press. Reprinted by permission of Carcanet Press Limited.

"A Weak Poem" by Roger McGough, from *Bad, Bad Cats* by Roger McGough, published by Puffin Books, 1997.

"A Poem" by Richard Meltzer, from *The Kingfisher Book of Comic Verse*, Roger McGough, Ed., published by Kingfisher Press, 1986.

"Cat Chair" by Chris Raschka. Copyright © 2001 by Chris Raschka.

"Easy Diver" by Robert Froman, from *Street Poems* by Robert Froman, published by McCall Publishing Co., 1971. Copyright © 1971 by Robert Froman. Reprinted by permission of Katherine Froman.

"Snake Date" by Jean Balderston. First published in *Light: A Quarterly of Humorous, Occasional, Ephemeral and Light Verse*, 1993. Reprinted by permission of the author.

"I Need Contact Lenses" by John Hegley, from *The Kingfisher Book of Comic Verse*, Roger McGough, Ed., published by Kingfisher Press, 1986.

"Eyelevel" by Ronald Johnson, from *Concrete Poetry: A World View*, Mary Ellen Solt, Ed., published by Indiana University Press, 1970. Reprinted by permission of Indiana University Press.

"Skipping Rope Spell" by John Agard, from *No Hickory, No Dickory, No Dock* by John Agard and Grace Nichols, published by Candlewick Press, 1995. Copyright © 1991 by John Agard. Reprinted by permission of Candlewick Press.

"Queue" by Sylvia Cassedy, from *Zoomrimes: Poems about Things That Go*, published by HarperCollins, 1993. Copyright © 1993 by the Estate of Sylvia Cassedy. Reprinted by permission of Ellen Cassedy.

"Eskimo Pie" by John Hollander, from *Types of Shape* by John Hollander, published by Yale University Press, 1991. Copyright © 1991 by Yale University Press. Reprinted by permission of Yale University Press.

"Popsicle" by Joan Bransfield Graham, from *Splish Splash* by Joan Bransfield Graham, published by Houghton Mifflin Co., 1994. Copyright © 1994 by Houghton Mifflin Co. Reprinted by permission of Houghton Mifflin Co.

"No Pretending" by Robert Froman, from *Street Poems* by Robert Froman, published by McCall Publishing Co., 1971. Copyright © 1971 by Robert Froman. Reprinted by permission of Katherine Froman.

"She Loves Me" by Emmett Williams, from *Speaking Pictures: A Gallery of Pictorial Poetry from the Sixteenth Century to the Present,* Milton Klonsky, Ed., published by Harmony Books, 1975.

"Sky Day Dream" by Robert Froman, from *Seeing Things* by Robert Froman, published by Thomas Y. Crowell, 1974. Copyright © 1974 by Robert Froman. Reprinted by permission of Katherine Froman.

"Crickets" by Aram Saroyan, from *Concrete Poetry: A World View,* Mary Ellen Solt, Ed., published by Indiana University Press, 1970. Reprinted by permission of Indiana University Press.

"The Salmon" by Douglas Florian, from *In the Swim* by Douglas Florian, published by Harcourt Brace & Co, 1997. Copyright © 1997 by Douglas Florian. Reprinted by permission of Harcourt Brace & Co.

"The Sawfish" by Douglas Florian, from *In the Swim* by Douglas Florian, published by Harcourt Brace & Co., 1997. Copyright © 1997 by Douglas Florian. Reprinted by permission of Harcourt Brace & Co.

"Swan and Shadow" by John Hollander, first published in *Poetry* magazine 1966. Copyright © 1966 by the Modern Poetry Association. Reprinted by permission of the Editor of *Poetry.*

"Forsythia" by Mary Ellen Solt, from *Concrete Poetry: A World View,* Mary Ellen Solt, Ed., published by Indiana University Press, 1970. Reprinted by permission of Indiana University Press.

"Whee" by Robert Froman, from *Seeing Things* by Robert Froman, published by Thomas Y. Crowell, 1974. Copyright © 1974 by Robert Froman. Reprinted by permission of Katherine Froman.

"Balloon" by Colleen Thibaudeau. Reprinted by permission of Colleen Thibaudeau.

"Giraffe" by Maureen W. Armour. Reprinted by permission of Maureen W. Armour.

"Acrobats" by Ian Hamilton Finlay, from *An Anthology of Concrete Poems,* Emmett Williams, Ed., published by Something Else Press, 1967. Copyright © 1967 by Ian Hamilton Finlay.

"Tennis Anyone?" by Monica Kulling. Copyright © 2001 by Monica Kulling. Reprinted by permission of Marian Reiner for the author.

"Pattern Poem with an Elusive Intruder" by Reinhard Döhl, from *An Anthology of Concrete Poems,* Emmett Williams, Ed., published by Something Else Press, 1967. Copyright © 1967 by Reinhard Döhl.

oo. La la la la
m. La la la la
um. La la la la
a la la. Tra la
a la la la. Ye